Understai Anglican Worship

A Parish Study Guide

David Kennedy

Rector of Haughton-le-Skerne, Darlington

GROVE BOOKS LIMITED
BRAMCOTE NOTTINGHAM NG9 3DS

Contents

Acknowledgements

I would like to express my gratitude to members of the Group for the Renewal of Worship for their comments on different stages of this booklet, and in particular Carolyn Headley, Janet Henderson, Christopher Cocksworth and Phillip Tovey. I am also more than grateful to Brian Hall for his suggestions and comments.

The Cover Illustration is by Peter Ashton.

1
Drawing Near to Worship

When Christians come together to worship, we offer our minds and bodies, our senses and imaginations, to bring to remembrance and contemplate God's love and goodness. We set apart, or consecrate, time to seek God's presence and in doing so there is a meeting, an encounter, an exchange; God draws near to us as we draw near to him, and the encounter is life-giving. God speaks, inspires, forgives, and renews our vision, and in response we express our praise and thanks, our needs and hopes, our faith and struggles. In this we employ the raw materials of worship, Scripture, prayer texts, symbol and ceremonial, hymns, psalms and spiritual songs, words and actions to express a mystery far beyond our capacity to grasp in order to articulate a common response.

Remembrance, contemplation, encounter, response. Anglicans have a rich inheritance of reflection upon these things, as the central historic formulary of our Church is not a creed or confession but a Prayer Book. Worship stands at the heart of Anglican self-identity. Moreover, the Anglican approach to worship has developed over 400 years, adapting and changing, and embracing a wide diversity of insight and styles. However, there are a number of elements that may be considered as characteristic of the Anglican ethos of worship and it is these elements that this booklet wishes to explore. One of the most pressing concerns for any church is the quality of worship and how we are enabled to get the most out of our worship. Careful personal preparation, a sense of expectancy, and openness to the leading of the Holy Spirit will take us a good part of the way. But there is also the question of what level of understanding and awareness do we have of the reasons why the style of worship is as it is? This is a particular issue for Anglicans who have an inherited pattern of liturgical worship, elements of which are prescribed and for that reason expected. The Church of England is also a church rooted in history with an inheritance from the past which has formed large aspects of Anglican identity.

This booklet is written in the conviction that our enjoyment of worship is strengthened by the kind of awareness we bring to it. We are often tempted to think of worship in terms of what we can get out of it. But this is only part of the issue. We bring to worship, not only a conviction that God will meet us, but also levels of awareness and understanding which inform, under-pin, and validate what we experience. If either expectancy or awareness is missing it is not surprising that worship can be perceived as dull and uninspiring. St. Paul in Romans 12 encourages us to be transformed by the renewal of our minds. What active awareness can we bring to enable us to get the most out of our particular Anglican pattern and style of services? Contemporary Anglicans perhaps show a tendency to take their tradition for granted, or at least fail to reflect sufficiently upon it. Another factor is that since liturgical renewal in the Church of England began in the 1960s, new services have tended to 'drop out of heaven' without, I suspect, much teaching and training to explain their rationale or how they might be presented.

Many of the issues discussed here are shared by other Christian traditions; little is distinctively Anglican, except perhaps for the particular combination and synthesis that we find in the public worship of the Church of England and the setting in which that worship is offered. Each section concludes with a series of questions, as it is suggested that this booklet might form the basis for discussion in Church Councils, home-groups, or worship committees.

2
Three Basic Convictions

i) Anglican Worship Gives a Central Place to Scripture

John Wesley wrote:

'I believe there is no Liturgy in the world, either in ancient or modern language, which breathes more of solid, Scriptural, rational piety, than the Common Prayer of the Church of England.'[1]

While the quotation has made many a Methodist blink in disbelief, it cannot be doubted that Scripture stands at the heart of Anglican worship. This is true not only in the way in which provision has been made for the public reading of Scripture at all Anglican services, but also for the way in which Anglican liturgical rites themselves are permeated by quotations from and allusions to the scriptural text. Even a cursory reading of the *Alternative Service Book* could leave no one in doubt that Anglicans are serious about Scripture. If anything, this tradition has been expanded in such recent liturgical reports and publications as *Patterns for Worship, The Promise of His Glory, Enriching the Christian Year,* and *Celebrating Common Prayer,* especially in the provision of biblical canticles and responsories. Used fully, the Anglican tradition steeps its worshippers in Scripture. This recognizes that there is much in the biblical record that of itself is highly suitable for worship in the articulation of truth about God or the human response to God's grace.

From the Reformation, the reading of Scripture in the vernacular has been a constant feature of the Anglican tradition. Archbishop Cranmer worked to a

---

1   Cited in Rupert Davies and Gordon Rupp (eds). *A History of The Methodist Church in Great Britain, Vol I* (Epworth Press, London 1965) p 261.

particular principle, outlined by Professor Oliver O'Donovan:

'…one of the earliest acts of the Henrician reform was the placing of an English Bible in churches; and that Cranmer's famous preface to the 1549 Prayer
Book was principally concerned with defending the reform of the lectionary
and Psalter—the ordered reading of Holy Scripture, rather than the exposition of it, being the centre of Anglican worship. Scripture is independent of,
and prior to, the church's exposition of Scripture, and the Church relates to
it, in the first place, simply by reading it aloud and only secondly by preaching.'[2]

This principle was criticised by the Puritans who insisted upon no Bible reading without exposition. Their point was that misinterpretation was a real possi-
bility, whereas a godly and learned Minister had the responsibility of 'rightly
dividing the word of truth' (2 Tim 2.15, AV). The Anglican approach, however,
has a higher doctrine of the congregation! Or at least it recognizes that, in the
corporate setting of worship, a responsibility rests upon the congregation to
hear and receive God's word. This process is aided, but not eclipsed, by preaching. The principle can be seen in the ASB rites where the versicle and response:

This is the Word of the Lord

Thanks be to God

—recognizing that Scripture is a divine gift to the Church and that God speaks
through the reading of it—is followed by a rubric suggesting a period of silence
so that together the congregation may reflect on the scriptural text. Allied to this
is the Anglican commitment to reading Scripture comprehensively. Non-Angli-
cans often express their astonishment that at morning or evening prayer on
weekdays, the psalmody, Old Testament and New Testament lesson have no
link because of this continuous reading principle. A responsibility lies on the
congregation to allow Scripture to speak to Scripture, grace relate to law, judge-
ment to mercy, puzzlement to assurance. 'You have heard that it was said by
them of old…but I say…' Bishop Stephen Sykes sees this corporate responsibility of attending to Scripture in an open environment as constituting an important locus of Anglican authority.[3]

The point is that in the public reading of Scripture, the role of the congregation is active, not passive, in which all are invited to submit to, wrestle with and
discern God's word. The fact that the readings are surrounded by canticles of
praise and prayers underlines the fact that God is to be trusted and his word
received in a context of praise and thanksgiving. On Sundays, the use of the
lectionary, and the advertisement of the readings for forthcoming services, means
that part of what we can bring is our own prior reflections on the readings.
Some churches use home groups and other mid-week meetings to prepare for
Sunday worship in this way.

---

2 *On the Thirty Nine Articles* (The Paternoster Press. Exeter 1986) p 50.
3 *The Integrity of Anglicanism* (Mowbrays. London/Oxford 1978) p 90ff.

ii) Anglican Worship Witnesses to the Importance of the Holy Communion

One of the most evident fruits of 20th century liturgical renewal is the understanding of the complementarity of word and sacrament. This came to fruition in the Roman Catholic Church, where the emphasis traditionally fell on the sacraments, through the Reforms of Vatican 2. Section 51 of *The Constitution on the Sacred Liturgy* decreed that 'The treasures of the Bible are to be opened up more lavishly so that a richer fare may be provided for the faithful from the table of God's word'. Consequently, the revised order of Mass includes a full ministry of the word (Old Testament lesson, psalm, New Testament lesson, Gospel and sermon), as well as the ministry of the sacrament. In Anglicanism, where until this century the emphasis traditionally fell on the word through morning and evening prayer, the Parish Communion movement restored the place of the sacrament but once again with the clear conviction that word and sacrament belong together. Of course, the idea is not new; it clearly was taken for granted in primitive Christianity. Justin Martyr describes the Sunday worship of the Roman Church in AD 150 where there were readings from both the Old and New Testament, a sermon, common prayers and then the eucharistic thanksgiving over the bread and wine. At the Reformation, Archbishop Cranmer, like other great reformers such as Martin Luther, Martin Bucer and John Calvin, desired a weekly communion service, and Cranmer's pattern for Sunday morning—morning prayer, litany and holy communion (with sermon), while long-winded, gave full expression to the need to be fed by Scripture and sacrament. Moreover, baptism was to be administered at a public service so that the newly baptized could be received by the congregation and to enable the congregation to be reminded of their own baptism and so of their commitment to Christ.

The restoration of weekly communion as a main act of worship in the Church of England in this century is therefore in total conformity with the scriptural, catholic and reformed emphases within Anglicanism.[4] But what spirituality do we bring to our eucharistic worship? Perhaps some of the resistance to the centrality of holy communion in some sections of the Church could be reduced by reflecting further upon eucharistic spirituality. The following suggestions would reward exploration.

The first is that holy communion has always centred on the presence of Jesus with his people. Although the mode of that presence has been an area of fierce dispute (the classic catholic position stressing the presence of Christ in the consecrated elements, while, for example, Cranmer stressed the spiritual presence of Christ in the heart of the believer), the focus of the service is communion with Christ, risen from the dead, generously bestowing on us his grace, forgiveness, strength, peace—indeed, all the benefits of his passion.

The second is that the eucharist continually keeps before the Church the

---

4   See Colin Buchanan, *The Heart of Sunday Worship* (Grove Worship Series 121; Grove Books Ltd, Bramcote 1992) for background and rationale for the centrality of communion.

central acts of our redemption, the dying and rising of Jesus. With this comes an appreciation of the cost of our redemption as well as the benefits that we have received, so that the natural response is gratitude, the loving thankfulness of those who know themselves to be bought with a price by an act of God's sheer generosity and love. It was the power of the administration of the elements as a visible and sensuous demonstration of God's free grace to sinners that led John Wesley to view the eucharist as a 'converting ordinance' as well as a confirming ordinance. The communion is able to bring people to Christ because it is a powerful demonstration of Christ's love. It is the stress both on Christ's presence and the depth of his grace that marks the administration as time for wonder and awesome contemplation.

A third is the place of thanksgiving. It is noticeable how thanksgiving is central to St. Paul's spirituality. Even when, as in Corinth, churches need to be recalled to apostolic doctrine and practice, Paul begins with thanksgiving (1 Cor 1.4; see also Rom 1.8; Phil 1.3; Col 1.3; 1 Thess 1.2; 2 Thess 1.3). The injunction to be thankful occurs regularly in Paul's writings (Phil 4.6; Col 2.7, 4.2; Eph 5.20). Modern eucharistic worship places thanksgiving at the centre—thanksgiving to God for his love in creation, redemption and sanctification. The intercessions also invite us to bring our thanksgiving as well as our supplication. To give thanks transforms our attitudes, owning our dependence on God and encouraging us to look for what is good and praise-worthy in others. We may wonder how churches and lives might be transformed if this spirituality was actually lived!

The fourth is our relationship with each other. The eucharist is a powerful demonstration of the same grace of God bestowed equally on each. Modern eucharistic rites have been constructed on a clear understanding of the church as the body of Christ, sharing the same faith (the change in the creed from 'I believe' to 'We believe' is significant here), together making the great thanksgiving (the eucharistic prayers are couched in the plural—'let us give thanks to the Lord our God', 'we celebrate', 'we proclaim', 'we make the memorial'). Moreover, the restoration of the peace not only makes explicit the intimate link between baptism and participation in the eucharist (in the second of the texts at section 30 of Rite A)[5] but also reminds each congregation of the gospel imperative for reconciliation and unity, of which the sacrament is the pledge and the seal.

The fifth is mission, expressed by the words of the post-communion prayers:
'May we who share Christ's body live his risen life; we who drink his cup
bring life to others; we whom the Spirit lights give light to the world.'
and
'Send us out in the power of your Spirit
to live and work to your praise and glory.'

---

5 See also section 1:10-14 and section 3:6 of David R Holeton (ed). *Christian Initiation in the Anglican Communion: The Toronto Statement 'Walk in Newness of Life'* (Grove Worship Series 118; Grove Books Ltd. Bramcote 1992).

Christian worship can always run the risk of self-indulgence and betray a tendency for congregations to look in on themselves. One test is the kind of issues we choose to pray about. The pattern of general intercession of page 125 of Rite A is comprehensive and wide-ranging, embracing the needs of the world, the church, the local community, the sick, suffering, and bereaved. However, in my experience, times of extempore or open prayer at this point in the service often fail to be anything like as comprehensive. While eucharistic spirituality does have an important individual aspect, the eucharistic word 'my blood shed for you and for many' is a potent reminder that Christ's sacrifice was for the world. The post-communion prayers are a reminder that gifts in word and sacrament are for a purpose—to strengthen Christians in the task of witness and service. So we bring our desires and our need of grace to sustain us in the task.

The sixth area is our ultimate future. The eucharist is not only a sign of our unity in the Body of Christ with all who have partaken of the one bread throughout history—'Therefore, with angels and archangels, and with all the company of heaven...'—but the effectual proclamation of the Lord's death until he comes. History moves towards that coming, the in-breaking of God's Kingdom in its fullness and the final re-uniting of all God's people. Indeed the dynamic by which material bread and wine become our spiritual food and drink is itself the pledge of the transformation of all creation, the foretaste of the heavenly banquet in the experience of a new heaven and new earth. The sense of longing for, and praying earnestly for, the final breaking in of the Kingdom is part of the spirituality we bring.

iii) Anglican Worship has a Special Concern for the Building Up of the Body of Christ

Both convictions outlined above are part of the traditional Anglican stress on the building up of the body of Christ. 'Let all things be done for edification', as well as being a primary concern of St. Paul, also stands centrally in Anglican texts ancient and modern. The rationale for services in the vernacular and the simplification of the rites of the Church at the Reformation was in order that worship might be accessible, understandable, and able to instruct, remind and strengthen Christians in their discipleship and mission. Anglican worship at its best should still reflect these concerns. Liturgical texts have always had an important teaching element. While many Methodists comment that they receive their primary theology from hymns, Anglicans will want to bear witness to the liturgy as well as the hymn or song book. The eucharistic prayer itself is a powerful and often comprehensive statement of thanks and praise for God's love in creation and redemption. The new eucharistic prayers that have recently been presented to General Synod are good examples of texts written first of all as worthy vehicles of worship, but also in language that is colourful, imaginative and clear so that the worshipper is enabled to engage with the text and so be built up by it.[6] This traditional Anglican stress on the role of the liturgy in building up God's people has been complemented in recent years by the fact that the congregation itself plays a fuller part in leading worship. The concept of presidency builds in the understanding that while certain elements of worship properly belong to the president, he/she may delegate other parts to others. The charismatic renewal movement has integrated into Anglican structures times of ministry where each literally does contribute 'a hymn, an instruction, a revelation, a tongue, an interpretation' (1 Cor 14.26).

Questions for discussion

1. 'We have come together......to hear and receive his holy word'. What is the difference between hearing and receiving? How can silence to used to help us receive God's word in corporate worship?
2. Of the list of suggestions of the types of spirituality we may bring to holy communion, which ones resonate with you and which ones are you unsure about? Which ones are prominent in your worship; would you like to see the balance adjusted?
3. In what ways do liturgical texts, hymns and songs, and musical settings build us up in the faith?

3
The Setting of Worship

English Anglicans are fortunate in that they are the inheritors of a rich legacy of parish churches, embracing diverse styles of architecture. Of course, this legacy is not without its problems in relation to the maintenance and the mission of the Church.[7] While styles of building are hugely diverse, one uniting factor is that Anglican architecture at its best, both ancient and modern, points to God's transcendence. Its provides a worship space that witnesses to the greatness and glory of God, a God to be approached in awe and reverence, and therefore to the smallness of self. The Prayer Book texts have often been criticised for a preoccupation with sin and unworthiness. While this may reflect aspects of general medieval spirituality and the turbulence of 16th and 17th century life,

---

6   *Eucharistic Prayers: Report by the House of Bishops* (GS 1120, CHP 1994).
7   I have deliberately chosen to look at a positive aspect here, in full knowledge that some buildings are simply a drain on the Church's finances and mission, and some have no particular architectural merit. My point is more about the presuppositions about the kind of worship space Anglicans have come to expect and enjoy, rather than the difficult issues facing us about how we cope with our glorious and not so glorious inheritance.

nevertheless, they do witness eloquently to the fact that all have sinned and fall short of the glory of God. The architectural setting therefore contributes to a sense that when we come to worship we are confronted with God's greatness which becomes our focus leading us to see ourselves as finite, mortal, sinful yet loved and redeemed by God. The sense of space and height lifts us up to contemplate the things which are above. Anglicans ought to know something about humility before God!

Our architectural inheritance and the appointment of our buildings also bear witness to divine creativity through the medium of human skill and craftsmanship. The Oxford Movement and more recently the Charismatic Renewal have contributed to a new appreciation of the importance of colour and symbol. The true rationale for flower arrangements, hangings and frontals, banners, pictures, is as a witness to the character of the God we worship, so that to enter a church building means we are immediately reminded and confronted by aspects of the nature of the One we approach. After all, God is a God of immense creativity and the great descriptions of the worship of heaven in Revelation reflect this.[8] Often this will draw us into worship, by creating an atmosphere, focusing our thoughts, and underlining the themes of the particular season or service. Of course, for the sake of the mission of the Church, church plants and satellite congregations will not have what may be considered to be the luxury of a specially-designed building. However, Anglicans in these contexts who wish to take their tradition seriously, will endeavour to witness to God's transcendence by the creative and careful appointment of whatever worship space they have.

Then there is the importance of the central symbols of the faith in our churches, principally, the font, holy table, lectern and pulpit. These are the visible signs of grace, the visible and constant reminder of our incorporation into the Christian family and the sustenance of word and sacrament. Lord Coggan writes:

'The architectural arrangements and furnishings of a church building should clearly show to the eye the centrality both of the Word and the Sacraments. Anyone entering a church should at once be arrested by two things—the central importance of a table where the faithful are fed sacramentally and of a pulpit (and/or lectern) from which the Word is read and expounded. Emphasis on the one should not lead to the disparagement of the other, nor vice versa. True Anglicanism— I would dare to say, a true presentation of the Christian faith—is bi-focal.'[9]

While these furnishings have a clear and distinct function, they are not merely functional. They represent the heart of the faith and they are visible reminders that we need God's grace. They have a role to play whether they are being used or not. There would be nothing more absurd than to install a baptistry and then cover it with floor-boards as if baptism had no significance except when it was

---

8 See Trevor Lloyd, *The Future of Anglican Worship* (Grove Worship Series 100; Grove Books Ltd, Bramcote 1987), where this is expounded at length.

9 *The Sacrament of the Word* (Fount Paperbacks, London 1987) p 23.

being administered. If the holy table is to be the living sign of a primary means whereby God feeds his children, this significance may be diminished if it is used as a stand for the over-head projector! The abandonment of the pulpit can mean little more than a loss of confidence in preaching under the guise of a desire for informality. The dignity of church furnishings complements the dignity of the word and preaching, of baptism and holy communion.

Of course, it would be foolish to suppose that all of our inheritance is good and helpful. Convictions about the nature of worship change; few congregations today would choose to worship in serried ranks of pews, straining to glimpse a distant eucharistic president far off in the east, with visibility obscured by a heavy chancel screen! While sensitive re-ordering and common-sense decisions about how we appoint our services can go a long way, many Anglican congregations are caught up in compromise. Yet even here there can be a positive sense that a building has been the focus of centuries of devotion by people living in this locality, through change, revolution, plague, war, yet the worship of God has continued, founded on his changelessness. In this sense, even the heavy medieval screen can teach us something!

Questions for discussion:
1. What immediate impact/first impressions does your building have on visitors who come to worship?
2. To what extent does your building communicate a sense of awe and wonder? What can be done to increase this sense?
3. In what ways does your worship witness to God's creativity? Can this be done more effectively?
4. In what ways are your worship and architecture 'bi-focal'? Would you think an imaginative re-ordering could develop a better balance?

4
Liturgical Texts and Language

The liturgy of the Church is often regarded with ambivalence. Newcomers to Anglican worship sometimes ask why a church sings the Gloria in Excelsis every week or why we keep reciting the creeds. In some churches, the prayers from the book seem to be regarded as rather tedious requirements (because this is an Anglican church) dutifully to be got out of the way before the 'real' worship can begin. Some churches have virtually abandoned Anglican formularies altogether.

i) *Things Old and New*

The Anglican approach to liturgical texts is determined both by our history and by our understanding of the Church of England as 'part of the one, holy, catholic and apostolic Church'. The preface to the *Alternative Service Book* begins with the words: 'The Church of England has traditionally sought to maintain a balance between the old and the new' (page 9).

This tradition is inherited from Cranmer's liturgical style, in which he retained certain classical texts, texts which may be regarded as the 'common property' of the Church universal, while he adapted others, and wrote new ones.

The use of classical texts is not just tradition for tradition's sake. It comes rather from a sense of history and continuity. It also witnesses to the fact that the Church of England claims only to be part of the universal Church. Some of our liturgical texts therefore, as well as being worthy vehicles of Christian prayer in themselves, remind us that we are part of something much greater. Moreover, they remind us that the Church has witnessed to Christ over 2000 years and we regard ourselves as in continuity with those who have gone before us. Anglicans do not jump from the first century to the end of the twentieth as if nothing worth considering happened in between. If worship is essentially our response to God's revelation of himself, we recognize in historic texts a common and true response to revealed truth.

Some Anglican texts can be regarded as historic-ecumenical. From morning and evening prayer, such would include:

-The recurring Trinitarian doxology 'Glory to the Father, and to the Son, and to the Holy Spirit...' (Gloria Patri), dating in its present form from the 6th century, but traceable to the second century.

-The canticle 'You are God and we praise you' (Te Deum), a Latin hymn probably originating in the 4th century.

-The Apostles' Creed, an early Christian confession, possibly in the context of baptism, introduced into the office in the 8th century.[10]

---

10 The word 'office' comes from the Latin for 'duty' and is used particularly of daily non-sacramental services of the word such as morning and evening prayer.

And from the eucharist
- 'Glory to God in the highest' (Gloria in excelsis), a 4th century Greek hymn originally used at morning prayer but introduced into the eucharist in the west at the beginning of the 6th century.
- The Nicene Creed, adopted by the ecumenical Councils of Nicea and Constantinople, regarded as the orthodox credal statement par excellence by many Trinitarian churches, and used in eucharistic worship since the 5th century.
- 'Holy holy, holy Lord' (Sanctus), while its Christian liturgical origins are uncertain, it has, since the fourth century, become an almost universal doxological component in the eucharistic prayer.

Many of the above texts originated before the schisms which have so fractured the body of Christ. By using them in worship, Anglicans assert their fidelity to historic traditions of the faith and their commitment to ecumenism. In the 1960s the work of the ecumenical group ICET (International Consultation on English Texts) produced a common translation of historic texts to be used throughout the English speaking world as a sign of common inheritance. This has enabled, for example, musical settings to be used across denominations. The fact that historic texts are used by Orthodox, Roman Catholic, Anglican, Lutheran, Methodist and Reformed Christians (albeit with different levels of regularity) means that components of worship are readily recognizable across the divides of language.

Other texts can be regarded as historic-Anglican. We could include here:
- The collect for purity ('Almighty God, to whom all hearts are open...'), translated from the private prayers of the priest before mass in the medieval Sarum rite, and incorporated into Cranmer's 1549 communion service and subsequent Church of England revisions.
- The prayer of humble access ('We do not presume to come to this your table...'), probably written by Cranmer and first included in his 1548 Order of Communion and retained, in different locations, in subsequent revisions.
- The general thanksgiving (ASB, p 104, 'Almighty God, Father of all mercies, we your unworthy servants...'), written by Bishop Edward Reynolds, Bishop of Norwich from 1661-1676.
- The third collect at evening prayer ('Lighten our darkness, Lord, we pray...'), translated by Cranmer from the office of compline (night prayer) in the Sarum Office Book.

Here we see the clear employment of things old and new; old Latin and Greek texts and prayers rendered into memorable prose and new prayers crafted by masterly writers of English.

In recent liturgical publications we see texts borrowed and adapted from other Christian traditions and also from sister Churches of the Anglican Communion. In *Lent Holy Week Easter: Services and Prayers*, there is a creative use of material from the Roman Missal, the BCP of the Episcopal Church (USA) and the ecumenical Joint Liturgical Group publication *Holy Week Services*. *The Promise of His Glory* incorporates texts from Anglican Provinces (USA, Canada, New Zealand, South Africa), as well as Roman Catholic, Orthodox, Methodist, and Reformed sources. It is likely that such borrowing will be an increasingly important feature of ecumenical partnership, while liturgical revision just beginning in Anglican Churches in Africa and Asia is sure to influence European and North American Anglican Churches in the future.

The aim in all of this is to give continuity and solidarity with the past with a shared inheritance in the present. Seen in this light, part of the spirituality we can bring is a welcome embracing of elements from the historic and contemporary situation, ecumenical and Anglican.

The same principle holds good for music. While the Church of England has never authorized a hymn book, there can be no doubt as to the importance of hymns and songs in Anglican worship. But if the principles applied to the liturgy are applied to music, Anglicans will want to draw widely using things old and new. Indeed, Anglican authors and musicians have themselves made and will continue to make a notable contribution to the repertoire of the universal Church. It would be a tragedy if some of the most profound poetry was lost to the Church simply because it is found in a hymn book rather than on an acetate sheet, or conversely, if the modern worship song was ignored or disparaged because it isn't traditional. Music, of course, witnesses to the doxological nature of many of our liturgical texts. It can be monotonous to recite Gloria in excelsis week by week, but to sing it can transform the text and enable it to be much more tolerant of repetition. Indeed, sung settings often become so popular that congregations regard it as a deprivation to have to do without them!

'Things old and new' also embraces other factors than texts and music. It is a fact that in the second half of the twentieth century, Christians of diverse traditions have come to value more the tradition of free and extempore prayer. Modern Church of England rites provide a clear framework in which there is a mixture of prescribed texts and permissive rubrics. Anglican worship style has shown itself quite capable of incorporating times of extended praise, open prayer, silence, or the exercise of spiritual gifts. It is of note that some Free Church traditions which historically have eschewed 'set texts' have provided model texts for ministerial and congregational use. Anglicans, coming from a very prescriptive background, now find considerable liberty within liturgical structures. The recent authorization of 'A Service of the Word'[11] is a clear indication of the liberty now recognized in non-sacramental worship.

ii) *Appreciating 'Givenness'*

While the Reformation settlement through successive Acts of Uniformity imposed an almost complete centralised control over Anglican worship, the more

---

11 GS1037B - see Anne Barton, *All-Age Worship* (Grove Worship Series 126; Grove Books Ltd, Bramcote 1993) chapter 5.

flexible texts and structures of the 20th century still adhere to a principle that there is a 'givenness' about Anglican worship. Even the permissive rubrics of 'A Service of the Word' do not encourage a free-for-all. Indeed, part of the rationale behind the new rite was to try to ensure that in creative non-sacramental worship the Anglican style of public worship does not simply fly out of the window. In contrast to some other Protestant traditions, Anglicans have refused to invest all the responsibility for the form and style of worship in the presiding minister. While it can be argued that Anglicans have to search hard for opportunities for creative praying (as in the opening prayers of adoration and confession in a classic Free Church service of the word) nevertheless the 'givenness' of the liturgy helps to underline the fact that worship is God-centred and prayer-centred rather than minister-centred. Or at least it provides a corrective to an over-emphasis on personality or personal inspiration (or lack of it). Parts of the eucharistic rite, for example, the beginning:

Greeting; Collect for purity; Prayers of penitence; Gloria; Collect of the day

or the ministry of the sacrament:

Eucharistic prayer; Lord's Prayer; Breaking of bread; Invitation

are able to flow under their own momentum; here parts of the rite sustain us, we do not sustain them. The focus comes naturally on the sequence of prayers. The danger of vain repetition only occurs if worshippers do not make the prayers their own, if they do not actually 'pray' them. Saying prayers together also fosters a sense of unity and common purpose among the congregation, and gives ritual expression to the corporateness of the Christian assembly. While this is not the only means affirming this, it is a natural and appropriate means. We all, for example, show our solidarity in expressing our penitence and need for God's forgiveness, responding directly to the scriptural text: 'If we say we have no sin we deceive ourselves...'

The prescribed prayers and structures also provide a rhythm, a sequence which is understood by regular participation. Indeed we can regard Rite A for example as a series of units:

Introductory unit; Word unit; Intercessory unit; Eucharistic unit; Post-communion unit

This gives a sense of movement and progression and ensures that an act of worship is balanced in its use of praise, word, intercession, thanksgiving, penitence. To this can be added blocks of praise, testimony, or special acts such as baptism. Each unit has its own form and flow.

Moreover, familiarity can be liberating. The value of repeated texts and regular and familiar structures allows worshippers to have a sense of security, to learn prayers by heart so as not to need to be overly dependent on books, to enable a sense of rhythm. Words and phrases entering deep into the memory also provide a quarry for personal devotion. Like reading good poetry, in well-crafted liturgical texts we often see new insights that we hadn't really noticed before, while recurring themes or key words can be highlighted through preaching.

iii) Liturgical Language Style

Another issue is the style of liturgical language. While the style of modern liturgical texts has come in for some criticism, nevertheless modern Anglican liturgical texts have largely retained a language which while contemporary, is still deferential. A good example is the variety of ways in which God is addressed in the collects. The ASB has largely followed the pattern set by the BCP, which in turn reflects the older Latin liturgical books. They reflect a tradition that is careful to honour God's name. While the language may be regarded as formal, in many ways it is parallel to the warm and devotional yet equally deferential way in which God is addressed in many contemporary worship songs. It is perhaps in open prayer when sometimes there is a sense that God has been reduced to the level of our best chum! While Jesus used the homely title of *Abba* (as well as 'Lord of heaven and earth', 'Almighty Father') there is no suggestion of over-familiarity. It is significant that St Paul in all his Christological references uses phrases such as the Lord, Christ, the Lord Jesus, Lord Jesus Christ, Lord Christ Jesus, Jesus my Lord, rarely simply 'Jesus'. Paul's language is partly theological—the titles 'Lord', 'Christ' define what he believed about Jesus, but it seems highly likely that this is also the language of Paul's prayer; the honour he attributed to the Son of God, 'the image of the invisible God' (Col 1.15). In this sense, the deeply reverential language of Anglican worship is entirely biblical.

While the debate will continue about whether particular forms of expression are helpful or easily understandable in our diverse culture, the principle of retaining a style of language that witnesses to God's otherness and the need for human humility and reverence is surely sound. Indeed, the balance of prescribed texts for the whole Church, and more localized forms of expression (e.g. in the intercessions and areas where 'any suitable words may be used') is potentially very creative. The Anglican tradition will want to preserve a balance between prayers that are universal and agreed and those that are localized.

iv) Texts We Have in Common

A further factor is respect for united texts. Successive liturgical commissions and General Synods have proceeded on the grounds that, as far as possible, texts would only be submitted and authorized which could in good conscience be used by the whole Church. This has been important for Anglican unity but it only succeeds if worship leaders and congregations embrace the principle. In this sense there is a biblical and proper concern for the unity of the body. It is a case of looking to each others' interests and not merely to our own, with a recognition of the labour and care that goes into finding forms of expression that we can all agree.

Colin Buchanan has observed that the 'set texts' in an act of worship only occupy about 10 minutes of the worship agenda.[12] Of course, liturgical writers

---

12 Op cit. p 6.

must strive for excellence and the prose of Cranmer is a notoriously hard act to follow. But even then the words of the ASB preface remain true:

'…words, even agreed words, are only the beginning of worship. Those who use them do well to recognize their transience and imperfection; to treat them as a ladder, not a goal; to acknowledge their power in shaping faith and kindling devotion, without claiming that they are fully adequate to the task.'[13]

Questions for discussion

1. To what extent is there a balance of things old and new in the worship you experience?
2. How can we make the words of the liturgy become the vehicle of your own prayer and worship?
3. To what extent do you find helpful the mix of prescription and freedom in contemporary Anglican worship?
4. 'Look to each others' interests and not merely to your own…' (Phil 2.4): how does this principle impinge upon your worship?

5
Worship and Time

From the first English Prayer Book the principle of liturgical time has been central to Anglicanism. This can be understood in relation to three cycles:

i) Daily: morning and evening prayer, the spirituality of which can be encapsulated in the phrases, '…we thank you that you have brought us safely to the beginning of this day…' in the morning, and 'Lighten our darkness, Lord, we pray…' in the evening.

ii) Weekly: Sunday worship, the first day of the week, celebrating the resurrection, the gift of the Spirit, the great themes of creation and re-creation in Christ. Liturgically, this is associated especially with the celebration of the holy communion. Cranmer's clear intention, as we have seen, was for at least a weekly celebration on Sunday.

iii) Annual: the retention of the calendar with observance of the main seasons according to western usage: Advent, Christmas, Epiphany, Lent, Easter, Whitsunday, and the Trinity season, with provision for the commemoration of saints and great women and men of the faith.

13 *Alternative Service Book*, p 11.

Perhaps most Christians relate most easily to the weekly cycle, the place of Sunday as the Christian day, notwithstanding the assaults upon Sunday in our society. The daily cycle is receiving more attention in the Church, especially with the publication of *Celebrating Common Prayer*.[14] The annual cycle is well established in the catholic tradition, but is perhaps less prominent in evangelical circles, apart from the major festivals of Easter and Christmas.[15]

The value of such observance of times and seasons is that they enable worship to reflect differing moods and themes, as well as facilitating a reasonably comprehensive and systematic approach to the re-telling of the Christian story. Intimately bound up with the calendar is the lectionary and the use of seasonal propers.[16] Liturgical renewal in this century, and recent Anglican seasonal resource books, have brought much richer provision for the celebration of the seasons. Such provision helps us to remember. Indeed, the concept of remembering or *anamnesis*[17] unites all three cycles outlined above. The foreword to Dr. Marion Hatchett's comprehensive commentary on the 1979 Prayer Book of the Episcopal Church (USA) begins: 'Anamnesis is the antithesis of amnesia'.[18] Day by day, week by week, year by year, by progressing through the seasons, each with its own theological and devotional associations, we hear the story, and the whole of the story, lest we forget the story. Moreover, the story itself embraces different emotions from triumph and victory to desertion and forsakenness, meshing with the experiences of our lives and of our world.

Of course, the observation of the Christian year is not without its opponents. Paul's words in Colossians 2.16—'Let no one make rules about what you should eat or drink or about holy days or the New Moon Festival or the Sabbath' have been used by some to deprecate any notion of the church year. The Puritans rejected the idea of the church year as being prone to superstition. Observance has not always been strong in Anglicanism:

> 'When in 1863 Archbishop Longley complained to the Queen about the fact that the Prince of Wales was being married in the penitential season of Lent, she replied, "In my young days there was no Lent".'[19]

The fuller observance of seasons with attendant liturgical colours was a further legacy of the Oxford Movement. However, it is much more helpful to see the Christian year in the context of spirituality rather than law. Observing the seasons enables us to enter into the reality of the truths that are being proclaimed; to claim them once again for ourselves, to appreciate that through our baptism

14 See Christopher Cocksworth and Paul Roberts, *Renewing Daily Prayer* (Grove Worship Series 123; Grove Books Ltd, Bramcote 1992).
15 Pentecost is now getting much more of a plug through the 'On Fire' initiative.
16 The word 'proper' designates items such as the introductory sentence, collect of the day, readings, proper preface and post-communion sentence designated for particular Sundays or holy days.
17 Anamnesis is the Greek word 'remembrance' from Jesus' saying at the Last Supper, 'Do this in remembrance of me'.
18 *Commentary on the American Prayer Book* (Harper & Row, San Francisco 1980) p xi.
19 Robert E Dolman, 'How Anglicans Turned Methodists into Dissenters' (lecture at Queen's College, Birmingham on17/5/94).

Christ's story has become our story. That is why there is a natural drama in the breaking in of Christmas, the walking with Christ to Calvary, the wondrous joy of Easter morning, the waiting for and celebrating the gift of the Spirit at Pentecost, the longing for the consummation of all things in Christ at Advent.

Lent is a good example. Modern liturgical study has re-emphasized the rationale for Lent as a period of preparation for Easter rather than a devotion on Christ's 40 days in the wilderness. In particular, Lent is a natural time to focus on the cross. The ASB eucharistic lectionary centres directly on the Lord's cross and passion from Lent 3 and the readings for morning prayer read progressively through one of the synoptic passion narratives throughout Lent. The BCP (1961) lectionary provides progressive reading through a passion narrative at evening prayer. There has been concern that evangelical spirituality has rather lost something of its primary focus on the atonement. Lent provides a ready-made opportunity for sustained reflection. And it is here that the catholic tradition of 'giving things up' can be profitably related to worship. Where Lent is seen as a time of self-examination, self-denial and meditation on the wonder and cost of the passion, a style of worship which is genuinely reflective and devotionally based will enable a stunning and dramatically powerful shout of triumph at Easter springing from hearts that have been genuinely renewed through extended meditation on the passion. As Lent is a season, so Easter is a season extending to Pentecost, allowing extended reflection on the resurrection and the hope that issues from it. Of course all eucharistic worship takes us to the cross, every Sunday is a festival of the resurrection. In the spirituality of the daily office, each new day reminds us of the dawning of a new creation proclaimed in the early morning mist of Joseph's garden; each evening is an invitation for us to commit our spirits to the Father as Christ gave up his spirit on the hill of Calvary. The seasons however invite us into a deeper realization and actualization of the realities of redemption.

Such an appreciation of the spirituality of the Christian year demands careful preparation and creativity on the part of parishes and individuals. Our approach to festivals would be transformed if churches are prepared to sit down, discuss and pray through how a local congregation might observe and celebrate seasons and festivals, what kind of themes they will cover and what kind of mood is suggested by these themes. Issues of presentation, the use of creative arts, how they might be seen as a means of evangelization and of giving public testimony to the faith they proclaim will be part of the discussion.

Questions for discussion
1. How meaningful do you find the concept of the 'Christian year'?
2. What moods and themes are suggested by celebration of the following seasons: Advent, Christmas, Epiphany, Lent, Passiontide, Easter, Pentecost? How might these be expressed in worship?
3. In what ways can you enrich your worship by incorporating some of the positive ideas which emerge from questions 1 and 2?

6
Worship and the Local Community

I have stated earlier that there is much in Anglican architecture and liturgical texts to remind us of God's transcendence. Modern liturgical renewal has retained this sense but not in such an austere way as in the Prayer Books from 1549-1662. An understanding of the Church as the body of Christ engaged in God's mission in the world has reminded us of a right immanence alongside the transcendence. This is underlined by Anglican commitment to the parish. While the mobile and cosmopolitan nature of large towns and cities, the diversification of traditions within the Church of England, and the consumerist supermarket approach to worship on the part of some Christians have weakened the concept of 'parish church', nevertheless, commitment to the locality is still a strong aspect of a church's self-understanding. Indeed, it has been strengthened by the stress on geographical areas apparent in the church planting movement. And here the Church of England seeks to be truly incarnational and relates worship to the context in which a church building or congregation is set. Preaching has always had a key role here as we seek to discern how the word of God once given in a particular time and context can be applied to our time and context, and how the scriptural imperatives relate to the realities of our streets and houses, our work (if we are fortunate enough to have any), and the issues, both local and national which affect and shape our lives. But this also relates to how we pray. The suggested pattern of intercessions in Rite A invites us to pray specifically for our local community, in the section :

> Give grace to us, our family and friends, and to all our neighbours that we may serve Christ in one another and love as he loves us.

Many congregations pray in a systematic way for the streets and institutions within their parishes in the conviction that God is Lord of all and that his care extends to all people and to schools, factories, day centres, youth clubs, sheltered housing, recreational facilities, and so forth. The sections on the sick and commemoration of the departed also relate the act of worship to the needs and the pain of people to whom the Church has a ministry of care and comfort.

Another important factor is the tradition of 'public worship'. Anglican notice-boards advertise services; historically the doors have been open to all who wish to enter. The 'givenness ' of the liturgy has provided a familiar setting for people seeking Christian faith to grow in understanding and commitment. A lot of the demands for greater accessibility of Anglican worship have sprung from a strong desire to see people come to faith. Alister McGrath relates this understanding to the doctrine of the Church:

> 'Anglicanism has long been committed to an Augustinian, rather than a Donatist, view of the church—that is, to an understanding of the church as a "mixed body", including both believers and non-believers, rather than a "so-

20

ciety of saints", from whose ranks those who have yet come to faith, or whose faith is faltering or uncertain, are excluded as a matter of principle. Most Anglican clergy…are well used to the fact that their congregations include seekers, hangers-on and drifters, as well as committed believers. For the evangelical wing of the church in the past, this has been seen as an irritation. Now it is seen as a bonus, and is increasingly being recognized by evangelical Anglicans as a vitally important point of contact between the church and the world, allowing evangelism to proceed quietly and discreetly, without putting "seekers" under pressure of any kind.'[20]

Anglican worship thus allows space for the faith to be caught. Indeed, Anglicanism has evolved very different styles of worship all of which have evangelistic potential claimed for them. For some, encountering the eucharistic community with its clear invitation to 'enter into communion' virtually demanding a response has been important; for others, the 'roominess' of the offices has provided space to listen and grow, while for others, the highly accessible and evangelistically orientated all-age services have led into deeper commitment.

A further aspect of the tradition of Anglican 'public worship' is the role the Church plays on civic occasions such as Remembrance Sunday and popular festivals such as Mothering Sunday, Harvest Thanksgiving, and services at Christmas. While the degree to which these are observed differs throughout the country, they are still significant occasions in many areas. The opportunity for the Church to relate its worshipping life to the work of institutions such as local schools on Education Sunday, or hospitals at St. Luke's-tide or local politics if there is a Civic Sunday, or to environmental issues in One World Week can further underline what it means to be a truly incarnational Church, inviting local people, many of whom have only a residual Christian commitment, to engage with the Church and its worship. 'The Gospel and our Culture' programme, initiated by Bishop Lesslie Newbigin, has sought to begin to address a lack of confidence on the part of the Church that Christianity has an important role to play in the formation of the public mind, that the Gospel is 'public truth'. While worship is not the only means of giving a Christian perspective on these issues, it has a time-honoured place in the Anglican tradition and provides the opportunity of a Christian perspective in the context of the praises of God and the ministry of intercession.

Questions for discussion

1. In what ways does your worship relate to the neighbourhood in which you are set? Can this be done more effectively?
2. Augustinian or Donatist? Is Alister McGrath correct in his assertion and what are the implications for how you plan and present your worship?
3. How important do you regard the civic and 'folk' festivals to be? Is it helpful to see them as opportunities for presenting the Gospel as public truth?

20 *The Renewal of Anglicanism* (SPCK, London 1993) p 34.

7
From Cradle to Grave

On the one hand the *Book of Common Prayer* and the *Alternative Service Book* can simply be regarded as collections of services; on the other hand, they can be seen as providing a framework for life. This comes out most clearly in 1662 with its presuppositions of a settled Christian society. The main contents are:

1. Calendar of Sundays and holy days
2. Offices of morning and evening prayer
3. Litany, prayers and thanksgivings
4. Collects, epistles, gospels for holy communion
5. The holy communion
6. Baptism of children and those of riper years
7. Catechism
8. Confirmation
9. Matrimony
10. Visitation and communion of the sick
11. Burial of the dead
12. Thanksgiving of women after child-birth
13. A commination for use on Ash Wednesday
14. The psalter
15. Forms of prayer to be used at sea
16. The ordinal, or ordination services for bishops, priests and deacons
17. Accession service
18. The 39 Articles of Religion.

1-5 and 13, 14 provide materials for the worship of the Church in its daily, weekly, and annual cycles. The psalter, communion lections, collects and prayer provided a quarry for devotion once prayer books became readily available to lay people. 6,8,9,11 are the classic rites of passage for birth, puberty, marriage and death. 7 and 18 provide theological resources; the first is related to preparation for confirmation, the second to Anglican self-understanding as a Church both catholic and reformed. 10 and 12 provide pastoral rites related to child-birth and sickness. 17 relates to the role of the monarch in a national Church and 15 to our context as a maritime nation. 16 sets out the Church's ordering and understanding of its ordained ministry.

While the ASB is not nearly so comprehensive as the BCP, the two books clearly stand in relation to each other. Other Anglican provinces have followed this approach in their own prayer books. So we see the same comprehensiveness in service books issued in Australia (1977), the USA (1979), Wales (1984), New Zealand (1989), South Africa (1991), and Papua New Guinea (1991). Of course, the notion that the Prayer Book really stands for all this in the minds of the average churchgoer is romantic in the extreme. Nevertheless, there is an important symbolic value in that the blend of public worship, private devotion, rites of passage and theology witnesses to the fact that praying and believing, worship and discipleship, are intimately linked, and that the life of faith embraces all the changing scenes of life both in sorrow and in joy.

Perhaps most of all, it sets before the Christian the vision of the consecrated life. This encompasses once and for all initiation in baptism, daily praise, worship, attending to Scripture, and intercession; the weekly observance of Sunday; and the great turning points in life through birth and growth, marriage, sickness and finally death. 'A book for the journey' would be an accurate way of describing this element of Anglican tradition.

The Church of England is faced by the issue of how many books should replace the ASB. The sheer variety of contemporary Anglican worship and of the resources available to service it makes the prospect of a single book a nonstarter. Recent General Synod discussion of the Liturgical Commission Report *One Book or a Series of Volumes in 2000* (GS 1114) affirms the principle of a core Sunday book for congregational use and a series of supplementary volumes for pastoral offices, initiation rites, daily prayer, and seasonal resources.[21] This makes sense, but in my view we would lose something important if the initiation (with rites for healing) and pastoral volumes became ministerial manuals rather than owned 'common prayer'. If Anglicans look to their liturgy to understand their theology, what the Church teaches about rites of passage, sickness and healing, reconciliation, is important. These are rites for the people of God not just the clergy. The Liturgical Commission is also considering the production of a 'knapsack' of prayers and devotions to help promote a common core of texts. Perhaps this will have a role in keeping the 'from the cradle to the grave' perspective as part of our liturgical heritage.

Questions for discussion:

1. 'The consecrated life'. To what extent do you think the Anglican tradition provides a framework for life and the journey through life?
2. Is it important that texts for the pastoral offices are accessible to Anglican Christians?

---

21 Of course the revolution in electronic technology could soon render such books obsolete, as parishes produce their own services from disc. Time will tell, although 'Green' sensitivities may well demand re-usable 'core rites' rather than wasteful weekly service booklets including liturgical texts, hymns and songs, lections, notices.

8
Bringing it all Together

This exploration of the kind of awareness or spirituality that we bring to worship has been painted on a broad canvas. It can perhaps be summed up as a series of balances: the balance between word and sacrament, Scripture and tradition; a right regard for history but the need to be contemporary; the balance between the aural and the visual, between transcendence and immanence, order and spontaneity, locality and universality. We see a conscious desire to aspire to a catholic spirit, arising from the self-identity of Anglicanism as part of the universal church, in which there is a right giving and receiving of each other's riches and insights into the mystery of Christ. All of this can rightly be claimed as part of our Anglican inheritance but it is also our challenge, not only in what the Church authorizes from the centre but how we order and present our worship in the local setting. But it runs deeper than this, for when we encounter God in worship and experience his presence, we grow in our knowledge of God, of the unity and diversity within the life of the Trinity, of God's changelessness but his immense creativity, his utter vastness and holiness yet his closeness and tenderness, of the eternal things which cannot be shaken yet also the new things into which God leads his people through his grace. It is the combination of order and stability, freedom and spontaneity, historical continuity with openness to new insights in our worship which enables us through our worship to grow in the knowledge of the God we approach. Anglicanism has a rich heritage in these things; as the Church of England moves towards the renewal of its worship for a new millennium, the task is for all of us to explore these things and so grow in awareness of what we are doing, for the sake of our enjoyment of our worship and fundamentally our growth in the grace and knowledge of the One to whom all worship and praise is due.